Nzinga D. Mpenda

Who Made the Potato Salad?

Celebrating the Journey of Black Womanhood

Copyright © 2018 [Get It Girl Publishing].
All rights reserved.

ISBN paperback edition: 978-1-7345270-0-1

Edited by Le'Jae Integrated Marketing, LLC

Brave Souls

Ebony Harris North Carolina
Edelena "CeCe" Smith South Carolina
Jessica Price Massachusetts
Latisha O'Brien California
Tanesha Hartsfield New York

Acknowledgements

Thank you to all of my queen sisters who graciously answered the call when I asked. You are the embodiment of grace and humility. This project would not have been successful without you.

To my queen sisters taking the journey and exploring the pages of this book, thank you! The journey has not been easy and the fight has not always been fair. I just want you to know that you are a powerful being that deserves to be celebrated. This is for you.

For our friends of various ethnicities and gender identities who will read this book, I say thank you. My hope for you is that you take a moment consider. Consider beyond your scope of comprehension. Consider your contention. And consider participating in this celebration of excellence. However, this party is not for you. This is our invitation for you to attend — as our guest. While reading, it is imperative that you remember you are a guest to this party.

Gratitude

I first need to thank God for if it weren't for Him none of this would be possible. From my life experiences to crowning my mind in creativity "Who Made the Potato Salad?" would not exist.

To my parents; I'm blessed to have you both alive and in reasonable. I love you.

To my siblings, family and friends who have supported me through this journey, you don't know how much I love and appreciate you. Life is more colorful because I have you to share it with.

To my editor, Tashiana, thank you for understanding me. The writer/editor relationship is one that I do not take lightly or for granted.

To the beautiful black women of the world, you are enough. Wear your crown with pride.

Who Made the Potato Salad?

Celebrating the Journey of Black Womanhood

Main Ingredients

The Recipe
Introduction
Meet the Queens

Black. Woman. Dope. (B.W.D.)
Where's My Black Girl Magic?
Black Support
Black, Unapologetically

Choosey Lover
Choosing Me: Dating
Choosing Me: Romantic Relationships
Choosing Us: Marriage

Working Woman
Unfair Advantage
Positions of Power
Stand Your Ground

Finding Peace
Stress Management
Rejection is Hard
Superwoman

Black. White. Society. (B.W.S.)

Black by the Numbers

White People

People of Color

Bowl, Lid, Spoon

Grab a Plate

THE RECIPE

Introduction

    Black women are remarkable and we should be celebrated more frequently. Our engagement with the world is so unique that only another black woman could understand our versatility and adaptability to the world for which we inhabit. We are the nurturers, providers, producers and the cornerstones from which all things are built. We are presented with good and make it great. We are given bones and make beautiful ornaments. We do not rest or settle until the world around us is at peace. We are dynamic.

    Black women are the backbone that this very nation was built upon. We birthed our children and fed the master's children from our breast. We are leached upon for direction and ridiculed for being too demanding. We are everything, yet simultaneously told at every corner that we are nothing. That our contributions are insignificant. That our feelings don't matter. And the only hedge of protection we have is from God, the Father, because for some of us, our natural fathers weren't present to protect us in the physical realm.

Society undermines and demeans us at every chance. But what I've learned is that people attack what they can't possess. And the only people that possess the spiritual power of *negroness* is the black woman. Our bodies are strong, our hearts are stronger and our resiliency is the strongest. They are angry at us because of all the things that they'll never possess.

We are God's gift to humanity — this is not insanity. Our blessings supersede all that can be touched because the more a possession is touched, the more it depreciates. We are untouchable. We are unmovable. Our place is cemented in the world's history and when they speak of all our accomplishments, we can relish in that victory.

My sister, I know life has been tough. I know you think that you've been dealt a bad hand, but through it all, you remain standing. It's time to refocus your energy. Ignore your fears and doubt. Address your pain, but don't allow it to overshadow your life. You are a queen, my sister, and as a queen, you must hold yourself to a higher a standard. Queens do not behave like peasants or entertain jokers. Queens move together fixing one another's crowns. A queen recognizes that there's space for all her queen sisters at the table and competition is only a distraction from running her queendom.

Meet the Queens

    I'm honored to present to you the amazing women who blessed my spirit by participating in this project and sharing their wonderful stories of challenges, recovery and elevation. As a black woman, circumstances aren't always kind and recovery from events that are beyond our control can be difficult to manage. These women have faced their fears, looked pain in the eyes and fought for the life they desired to live. A life filled with love, joy, adventure and peace.

    I met Jessica during second semester of my freshman year at Shaw University in Raleigh, North Carolina. Jessica was born in Mississippi and grew up in a Boston area suburb. When I met Jessica, I didn't believe that black people lived in Massachusetts. We met in a theater class; she was a theater major and I needed an elective. I don't quite remember how our friendship developed, but I'm glad that it did. When it comes to how she feels about being a black woman, Jessica shares: *"I feel like we are some of the most resilient and strong creatures God has created. Whenever I need inspiration, I look to the strong black women around me."*

Tanesha was my first friend in college. In fact, she was my only friend until I met Jessica. Tanesha is from Harlem in New York City. I'd never been to New York at that time but the culture of the Harlem Renaissance, Langston Hughes, Zora Neale Hurston and all of the writers, poets and musicians of that era always spoke to soul. Tanesha and I met because we were the only two day students in a night class for adults. It made sense that we clicked since I was from San Francisco and she was from NYC — two city girls among all of the country folks. As a mother of two daughters, Tanesha adds: *"We are fucking awesome and there is no one like us!"*

Edelena (or CeCe) was my roommate during my freshman and sophomore years. God places people in our lives intentionally. We became roommates because during freshman check-in, the dormitory was less than organized and I was literally standing behind her in line, waiting for a room key. CeCe is from Charleston, South Carolina and she was one of the most religious people I'd met at that time. I learned a lot about my own faith during our time together. Clearly God knew what He was doing. When it comes to making her mark in the world as black woman, CeCe shares: *"I want to be unforgettable. I want the world to know that we are our brothers' and sisters' keeper. I want the world to know that when I die, that I LIVED!"*

I can't recall how Ebony and I became friends. She was a year ahead of me in college and had a completely different friend group. We were both psychology majors and somehow, through the course curriculum, we became acquainted. Ebony and I are kindred spirits who believe in helping and providing for our families. Ebony believes: *"It is truly important to understand that as black women, we are constantly fighting uphill battles. They are never ending. We do not have to let our circumstances define our present, our future and our relationships. Nor do we have to exhibit behaviors/emotions that we feel inside, which ultimately confirms the negative perceptions that society already has of us. We rise above because we are truly queens and keep fighting when others cannot."*

I met Latisha while consulting with a local nonprofit in Oakland, California. Latisha had an amazing spirit and wonderful energy all around. There were many demands placed on her and many responsibilities that were outside of her scope of duties, and I watched how she masterfully managed it all. An artist herself, Latisha was the first person to call me an artist. I didn't see myself as one. I always felt that visual artists were the real artists. Latisha told me that I was an artist with words, but an artist nonetheless. We shared many stories during the time I worked at the organization. When I discovered Latisha's age and some of what she'd experienced, it confirmed for me that black women are, indeed, the light of the world. Latisha doesn't look like what she's been through and she's the embodiment of the colloquialism, *"Black don't crack."*

BLACK.

WOMAN.

DOPE.

Where's My Black Girl Magic?

Being a black woman is one of the toughest, yet most rewarding, experiences of my life. Due to my own insecurities, I haven't fully stepped into my power as a black woman, but the one thing I've learned is that how I view myself in the world is not the same as how others view me. In fact, others view me with high regard. I oftentimes appear a lot more confident and self-assured than how I truly feel. The blessing in having these feelings of inadequacy has been having a tribe to inform me of how amazing I am.

Going forward, the key for me is stepping into that awesome persona that the world has already assigned to me. In a world that praises productivity, it's easy to believe that you're not doing enough. I find it easier to support women in their endeavors. I'm always quick to cheer on another black woman for her accomplishments and aspirations. Although I believe every black woman (and girl) has magic, I have a

Notes: _____
_____
_____
_____
_____

difficult time recognizing my own. I don't view my own accomplishments or the way I show up in the world as extraordinary. Despite my flawed perception of myself, there are others that do see me as worthy of recognition. It's not that I need to manufacture my magic. I don't even need to go looking for it. I simply need to OWN it!

It was difficult for me to recognize my magic because I didn't fully understand what my magic was. I had to go to God the Source for clarity. What I learned is that my magic includes improving all that is around me. When I enter into a space, it's my job to make processes, functions and people better. This doesn't mean that I own people's actions or specific outcomes. It means that through my presence, I influence the space for the better. The second part of my magic is creating and facilitating opportunities for people to experience personal or professional growth. In retrospect, I understand that my magic isn't what I want it to be or based on my comfortability. My magic is already what GOD said it would be. Knowing this, I can walk in my magic more boldly.

Sometimes, our talents may elude us or we may need more time to feel confident in stepping into them. We all have talents that comprise our own unique

"Black Girl Magic." Jessica shares: *"I'm a creative and a healer. I've had the pleasure of helping coworkers, family and friends realize their dreams, heal and love. I encourage them to find the courage to live in their truths. I've also used my creativity to make creations (natural products) that improve my quality of life, as well as the lives of others."*

Sometimes our Black Girl Magic is a way of life or an extension of our legacy. Tanesha wants the world to know: *"That I was here. I want to be remembered throughout the ages. Not just two or three generations down the line and then forgotten."*

CeCe is living life out loud and sprinkling her Black Magic all over the world. CeCe shares her current list of priorities: *"First, creating a legacy! Creating a blueprint of success for myself and for others. Failure is not an option and ordinary is simply not good enough. I have too many ideas in my head to be ordinary. I've been blessed to live an amazing life so far and the only way from here is up. Second, 'To thou own self be true.' Living in the moment! Taking in the*

Notes: _____
_____
_____
_____
_____

fresh air! Smelling the roses! Life is too short and we forget to enjoy every part of the journey. Third, God, Gawd, Allah, the Father. Understanding how amazing the Father is through my willingness to see Him in all things and all people. Also, bringing healing to others through light and love. Fourth, faith over fear! I refuse to be trapped by any idea, job or relationship that isn't connected to faith! I am committed to taking risks, loving people and making decisions that scare me. Fifth, protecting my home and my peace! As I prepare to be a wife, I'm intentional about my friendships and connections. My home is my safe place and I refuse to let anyone destroy the foundation that I've built."

CeCe's Black Girl Magic takes form in a number of spaces: *"I've traveled to over 10 countries! Individuals from my part of town typically don't leave the city, let alone the country. I've started my second business. I'm still working on official launch logistics, but I'm so proud to embrace entrepreneurship and work toward creating wealth for my family. I didn't become a statistic. I graduated from high school and college without having a baby prematurely. My greatest accomplishment is that I'm creating a legacy for myself that embodies hard work, dedication and a made up mind."*

Ebony's discovery of her own Black Girl Magic comes through a note to her younger self: *"To my 18-year-old self, I would say, 'Girl, listen...you have to be strong and resilient. Some people will like you and some will not. At times, you will win and other times, you will lose. Always remember where you came from but do not let it hinder you from achieving your goals. Make acquaintances who are where you want to be because those are the people who will either help you get to where you want to be, or become the driving force for you to push yourself to get there. You can live life, have fun and be adventurous but always remember what your end goal is.'"*

Notes: _____
_____
_____
_____
_____

Black Support

You will not a find a more disrespected and unappreciated person in the world than a black woman. The magic that composes the essence of the black woman is both terrifying and fascinating to all others. Black women are often made to feel insignificant and minute regarding their natural existence from God. The glory of the black woman becomes evident when, at some point in her life, she recognizes her power and begins to live within it. A black woman who's had her essence cultivated since her birth is a wonderful thing. But for many of us, we must first learn what we are capable of, and then take a chance to live within that space. However, once a black woman has become self-actualized, it's truly a beautiful sight.

In today's landscape, black women are working both independently and collectively to achieve goals more than ever before. Some outliers certainly exist,

Notes: _____
_____
_____
_____
_____

but black women are becoming entrepreneurs, executive leaders and political influencers in unprecedented numbers. Throughout all of this, what's even more gratifying is how black women are *intentionally* supporting other black women. Black women have shifted from requesting a seat at the table to creating new spaces (and tables) for conducting business. Black women are rejecting the notion that it's necessary to "stay in your lane," which could arguably be the catalyst behind several advancements within our community. I believe black women inherently understand lanes are limiting and they fail to foster progress. I reject these lanes and I believe I am great company of many black women.

    As existing entrepreneurs, let's explore the respective journeys of CeCe and Latisha to learn how each woman arrived at her current place. Both women have a social service background, working with youth and young adults in various capacities. Both women expressed the desire to leave the institutional grind to build wealth and become their own boss. We're oftentimes warned that if we fail to follow our dreams, we'll spend the rest of our lives working toward someone else's.

Tanesha has a slightly different approach regarding what fuels her professionally. At the age of 19, Tanesha did something that wasn't common for people in her age group. After completing one year at Shaw University as a psychology major, Tanesha transferred back to a university in NYC to pursue an education in film. For Tanesha, being the first in her family to attend college was important, but so was pursuing a career that she loved. Instead of wasting time at a university that didn't offer what she needed, Tanesha boldly made the necessary moves to achieve her goals.

Based on her unique path to success, Tanesha shares her top five accomplishments: *"In no particular order...first, using my college degree. Too many people finish college and never use their degree. Second, having a career, and also having a plan and seeing it actualized. I'm very fortunate. Third, having two healthy daughters who love me and who think the world of me. They're my greatest creation and without them as motivation, I don't know where I'd be. Fourth,*

Notes: _____

_____

_____

_____

not going insane in a world that puts so many weights upon our shoulders. Basically, not giving up. Fifth, not allowing the thoughts of others to influence who I am. I march to the beat of my own drum."

It's not uncommon for black women to teach their daughters to sacrifice and "do what you gotta' do" to make things happen. For generations, black women have neglected themselves in various ways for the greater good of others — usually family — because the family unit was viewed as more important than individual success. Latisha reflects on her mother who sacrificed her health, well-being and self-preservation to meet the demands placed upon her: *"I think my awakening was seeing my mother, who always put herself last, struggle with debilitating back pain. However, her perseverance to carry on is breathtaking. My mother fell and broke her tailbone almost 50 years ago. She was unaware of her injury until she experienced back pain several years later. Several decades and two back surgeries later, she still has debilitating back pain. My mother recently expressed that she didn't want to stop working to see about herself. Wow! My mother has had to fight for almost everything her entire life. She's even taken care of two sisters and a niece with an addiction and mental health issues. Today, she uses a walking aid, but continues to struggle with allowing her body to rest. The last time I visited her, what resonated with me is the importance of saying, 'No' to family and friends who no longer serve you, and relinquishing the things that you can't control."*

According to CeCe, growing into black womanhood isn't always an easy transition since black girls don't get the care and attention deserving of their intelligence and innovation. Although most of our families do their best to love us and not intentionally harm us, the methods employed aren't always the greatest. CeCe describes her formative years: *"'Books and boys don't go together' was what my Aunt Nancy always said. I was one of the few to graduate high school and college. Many of my cousins ended up dropping out, getting pregnant or simply not pursuing anything further after high school. I was encouraged to pursue my dreams. My family honestly celebrated my success. I no longer believe that you can't enjoy both. Scholastic success is just as important as family and friendships."*

Notes: _____
_____
_____
_____

It's also important to note the importance of extended family. We can't control the circumstances that we're born into, but we must deal with the consequences nonetheless. It's a blessing when God brings people into our lives to ensure that we're properly nurtured and cared for regardless of familial or biological relations. Ebony shares how her family was instrumental in her life: *"Family was very important in my upbringing. I grew up in an extended family home, which included my paternal grandparents, dad, aunts, uncles and cousins. My grandfather passed away when I was younger. During this time, my older cousin and an aunt passed away, as well. My aunt's death was a big blow to my heart because, along with my grandmother, she was my protector. The two protected me from the hurt that I experienced from the rest of my family. My family was very close knit. My grandparents' home was the 'heart' of the family. Everyone met at my grandparents' house for daily gatherings. This is where everything happened, good and bad.*

My grandmother was a very strong woman. She held the family together and still does! She worked hard raising her children, then turned around and raised me, and three of my cousins. She also fostered three children, two of which had developmental disabilities. 'Strong' is truly an understatement for this woman. I received many of my values from her. My dad was also a strong man. He was a very hard worker. He held down really good jobs and maintained steady employment. I'm almost certain that I get my work ethic and strength from these two people."

Ebony elaborates on the love and support she received, which shaped her outlook on life: *"My biggest accomplishment is changing my attitude and beliefs about myself. My attitude was absolutely horrible and if I continued the way that I was headed, it would've been a tragedy. I was quick-tempered with no filter. I can truly say that it probably affected the degree of my success during my elementary, middle and high school years. Academically, I was a great student. But I became a bully at some point in high school. As I reflect back over the years, I realize it was a cover for what I felt on the inside: anger, hurt and a lack of control. Attending college, however, was a big change for me. I learned to tone down my anger as I entered the*

Notes: _____
_____
_____
_____
_____

professional work environment and interacted with people from various places. Completing my first degree was another huge accomplishment. I was so proud of myself. My grandmother, mom, dad, cousins and close friends all came out and supported me. It was pretty awesome! Being a strong, independent woman is something that I've always been proud of. I've fought through a lot of obstacles to get where I am and I've achieved so much. Although I may not be where I want to be, I've come a long way. I'm not afraid to love my fiancé, who I've had the pleasure of spending seven long years with."

Black, Unapologetically

Black women are leading the charge within our culture of being "unapologetically black." For too long, we, as black women, have had to shrink ourselves in order to make others feel comfortable in our presence. Ha! Our presence, in any space, is a gift to all those in attendance. Our creativity, leadership and ingenuity are the source of invention and innovation throughout our history. We're notoriously known for "making a way out of no way." Don't debate me. If you want to confirm this, ask a black woman to recall how her mother, grandmother or aunt managed to produce a lot with only a little, and, in that moment, how they and their family felt. Chances are there were feelings of joy, gratification and praise.

Indeed, black women are awesome. When was the last time you were around a group of black women and the atmosphere didn't feel "magical"? Dictionary.com defines the word "awesome" as

Notes: _____
_____
_____
_____

"causing or inducing awe; inspiring an overwhelming feeling of reverence [or] admiration." You'd be hard-pressed to find a black woman who *doesn't* illustrate this definition or evoke such feelings of the word. Older black women are especially magical considering all that they've endured and how they remain resilient and fearless. Older black women are the physical manifestation of God. (I'm not saying they *are* God). Considering God's expectations for how we should govern ourselves and treat one another with love and grace, older black women have it figured out. They're the women who refuse to be broken or embittered by life's circumstances, and those who're willing to pour their knowledge and wisdom into the younger generations. We affectionately refer to these women as "Auntie" or "Mama" depending on their age. Some of our favorite include Oprah, Michelle Obama, Viola Davis, Cicely Tyson and Jenifer Lewis. Of course, this isn't an exhaustive list as there are plenty of other aunties and mamas that we collectively love and adore.

At some point in her life, every black woman must decide to commit to her true, authentic self regardless of society's expectations or perception of her. There is a journey from being a black girl to living as a black woman, Jessica advises: *"Love yourself and believe in yourself. Don't let other people or fear stop you from being the best you that you can be. Be you unapologetically."*

As black women, we don't always feel that we have permission to live exclusively for ourselves. We oftentimes take on supportive roles for those we love and care about. On discovering challenges that impacted her ability to be her authentic self, Tanesha shares: *"Know that it's okay to say 'NO.' I think I'm a people pleaser and because of that, I try to appease everyone. I must understand that when I say 'yes' to one thing, I also say 'no' to something else. So, I have to make firmer 'noes' and be okay with it, and say 'yes' to myself more."*

Black women are responsible for the legacy we leave behind, so it's extremely important that we navigate in the world and make the appropriate adjustments. Latisha depicts her vision: *"I'm passionate about creating visual interpretations of beautiful stories, specifically of black women. I want to change the dynamic and the stereotype that black*

Notes: _____
_____
_____
_____
_____

women are oversexed, sharp-tongued and angry, and therefore, deserving of the bad things that happen to us. I incorporate hands in most of my artwork because our hands can do so many things. They can be a tool for healing or a weapon for abuse. I also incorporate braids and natural hairstyles in my work because hair is a tense issue for black women. Our natural hair is our birthright and it should be celebrated and displayed with pride in all forms. Community is essential, especially when family relations are strained or nonexistent."

It's essential that Black women learn to make ourselves a priority. Ebony explains the impact of prioritizing herself: *"Being the best me is the most important thing in my life right now. This has been a recent change because of the struggles that I've been through and continue to go through. Until recently, I've allowed anger to overtake me, control my emotions and alter my course in life. As selfish as it may sound, I've had to let go of some of the closest people and things in my life so that I could take this journey. My personal relationships are extremely important. Over time, I've learned that not everyone is good for you and not everyone has your best interest at heart. With that being said, I've had a very special person next to me for seven years, and although every moment isn't perfect, I've grown into a much better person. Although I've always felt like I was a strong woman, he's helped shape me into a person that's stronger and ready to fight against all that the world's been throwing at me as a woman of color, and us. In addition, completing my education is essential to me transitioning into the next stage of my life. The experience has grounded me physically, financially and emotionally.*

I want to leave a legacy that shows we can believe in others without the fear of being hurt or torn down. We can love, share, help and teach others the way our ancestors did. Peace and tranquility aren't dead. Harmony can be achieved. Through hard work and community, we can achieve without boundaries. I want my future family to have what their hearts desire without sacrificing their physical and mental health. And I want them to have an understanding and appreciation for those that worked hard to pave the way for them."

Notes: _____
_____
_____
_____
_____

CHOOSEY LOVER

Choosing Me: Dating

I'm the first to admit that I don't know how to date. Being single is so easy and comfortable. I do single very well. However, I eventually want to get married. In order to do so, it's necessary for me to engage in the struggle life of dating. I've never been a woman to bounce from man to man. I believe that your head and heart need time to reflect and recover in between relationships. There should be a lesson we can glean from our dating relationships which should ultimately make us a better person for ourselves and a better mate to our life partner.

Dating is awkward for me and for that reason I can only seriously invest my energy in one guy at a time. In 2018 I began dating this man, let's call him Brandon, whom I was familiar with. Brandon and I had a lot of parallels in our lives despite him being 10 years older than me. The age difference was a problem for Brandon though I believe he really wanted to move

Notes: _____

_____

_____

_____

past it. Our foundation was built on friendship – and to be honest that is where I should have left it – friendship. It wasn't long, maybe two months, that I begun to disconnect from Brandon and what he believed was our growing relationship. Initially, I intended to end things with Brandon and enjoy the single life. Being single is easy, comfortable and I know what to expect. I was faced with the decision to consider his feelings or to choose my happiness. At the time, I felt that I'd already done so much for others that it was time to do what was best for me.

  During my process of disconnecting from Brandon a new opportunity, with "Thomas" presented itself. Thomas wasn't on my radar, but he was a pleasant surprise. For reasons unbeknownst to me, the universe saw fit for us to connect. We had our bumpy points, mainly due to the fact that I prefer to know every detail at any given time. We both had to work around our comfort point and the needs of the other. We worked because Thomas was clear about what he wanted from life. I was pleased to find that we wanted the same things. Thomas shared with me early that he had everything he needed except for a family, wife and children. I was all ears. I'd never met a man so clear about what he wanted. On our first date, he spoke his intentions immediately and proudly. Yet, I wasn't sold on Thomas right away. It took me a few weeks to get a feel for him and monitor his consistency. I admit that I still didn't know how to date, but I decided that he was someone worth exploring further.

Raise your hand if you've ever heard your mom, aunt, grandmother or another family member say, "Those books better be your boyfriend!" The meaning behind this colloquialism is meant to encourage girls to focus on their education for bright and productive futures. Simply, the focus should be on personal growth and not on anyone else, especially boys. Though well-meaning, in childhood, the impact of those words can linger well into adulthood. Life is about exploring and that includes romantic relationships. Jessica reflects on the messages she received about dating during her childhood: *"My parents didn't let me date in high school. I was always told to not be 'fast' and focus on school. Like many black girls, I was told to wait until marriage to have sex,*

Notes: _____
_____
_____
_____

and that no man wanted to marry a woman who didn't respect herself (slept around). I was taught to cook and clean. I was constantly criticized about my size because 'men don't like fat women.' One scripture that was reiterated was that 'when a man finds a wife he finds a good thing' (Proverbs 18:22). So, I figured I should let a man find me and not go looking for one. I never realized how much [my family was] preparing me to be a wife rather than teaching me what to seek in a husband. I think it was good advice, but today is just a different time from when [our parents or grandparents] were younger. Things have progressed. My friends taught me to be more assertive while dating, but I'm still kind of reserved. I kind of wish dating was like when my grandparents met. Today, most men don't care if you can cook and clean, or how many people you've slept with."

Many of us view relationships as an opportunity to escape family dysfunction or create the family we've always wanted. Sometimes we use relationships to fill other voids in our lives. It's necessary that we guard our hearts while dating and with every relationship we decide to enter. Latisha shares advice for her younger self on romantic relationships: *"I would tell my 18-year-old self to 'stand in your truth!' Begin to root yourself in what you know is best for you whether it be relationships, food, or employment. Take your time, nurture and protect your heart. You're worth more than a handsome face and a broken soul. I married my first husband at 19, became a mother at 20 and was divorced by 21. I think under the circumstances, I married my first husband for security and stability. Even in the midst of adversity, I say, 'stand in your truth' and follow your gut.*

Explore the goodness of people by traveling to different lands and exploring different cultures to see the world through unfiltered eyes rather than what's manufactured in the news. Explore nature by planting something beautiful. The size of the container doesn't matter; begin the process of planting so you can connect to nature and appreciate how life and beauty begins with a seed. Choose your friends carefully. Friends should nurture you regardless of circumstances. Friends who are genuine will always circle back even when there is strife."

Many black families hold religion sacred and use

Notes: _____

_____

_____

_____

_____

it as the guiding force to deter black girls from dating and entering romantic relationships. As the daughter of a preacher, the stakes were even greater for CeCe. She describes how her family dealt with dating and sex: *"I never really had a conversation about relationships and sex. The message was only conveyed from the pulpit that if I got pregnant before marriage, I'd end up embarrassed in front of the entire congregation. Intimacy was never a topic of discussion. I figured everything out by trial and error."*

While premature pregnancy and the fear of our black girls becoming distracted are legitimate concerns, it's equally important that we teach our black girls how to date and equip them with the necessary tools to protect themselves against unproductive and harmful relationships. We must show them how to value themselves while pursuing romantic interests. We should answer their questions and hear their concerns without judgement. Intimacy and romantic relationships are a natural part of the human existence. We place our black girls at risk of venturing down unknown paths by failing to embrace and acknowledge the role of dating and relationships.

Choosing Me: Romantic Relationships

    I knew it wouldn't work between Brandon and I when he conveniently left his wallet at home on our second date. We attended a holiday play that evening and he was driving back to my house to drop me off. About halfway there, he indicated he was hungry. I'm not sure why he said anything, knowing that he didn't have any money. I wasn't hungry and hadn't mentioned food. However, as a kind gesture, I offered to buy him food. I blame my mother for my bleeding heart. He declined my offer perhaps because he'd have to eat alone.

    Things became more interesting as we approached the toll plaza and he expressed that he didn't have toll money. Really, dude? You live in "the City" (San Francisco) and I live in the East Bay so, of course, you should've known that you'd need five dollars to get home. I was flabbergasted. Nevertheless, I offered to give him the toll money. He initially

Notes: _____
_____
_____
_____
_____

declined but accepted. He then asked me for ten dollars and said he'd pay me back via PayPal. I only had twenty-dollar bills in my wallet, so I gave him $20 when we reached my house and exited his vehicle. He never paid back the money. I would've reminded him, but I don't believe that I should have to remind someone that they owe me money. They know. They simply choose to pretend like it didn't happen.

  Against my better judgment, I continued to see the Brandon. I was bored and he was available. I *wanted* to give him a chance although I kept telling my friends that he wouldn't make it past the new year – it was December – we had only been exploring a relationship since mid-November. My friends insisted that I shouldn't cut men off so quickly. Actually, I should. However, I wanted to be more open and not write a guy off based on one infraction. One thing I learned is that friends mean well, but they can still provide bad advice. I love my friends, but when it comes to my romantic relationships, my voice is the only voice that matters. This is one reason why I don't share my romantic life with others prematurely. I'm able to determine whether or not things will work out between me and a potential guy, so I don't see the point of exposing my family and friends to them unless they're going to be around.

Back to Brandon. For the most part, things were smooth. Unfortunately, we disagreed on a lot of things — respectfully, but we didn't see eye-to eye nonetheless. I wanted marriage and he was vehemently against it. I accepted his truth and knew that we were only biding our time. There's no way I could wait for a man to potentially change his mind about marriage. Again, I was bored and he was more than available. Dating him gave me the opportunity to practice new approaches of femininity and vulnerability. These aren't my strengths and I recognized that as a woman, I needed to "soften up" a bit. He was great teacher in that aspect. I could trust him in that way. We were growing a solid friendship and, honestly, that's where it should've stayed. We dated a few weeks longer and by then, I was completely over him as a man. There was no way we could progress romantically because I didn't respect him. Money isn't everything in a relationship, but it's

Notes: _____

_____

_____

_____

_____

certainly important. I don't ask for a man to break the bank for me or even go beyond his financial means. What's absolutely NOT acceptable, however, is any grown man waiting and expecting for me to pay his way. It's not going to happen. The second that I find myself having to use my resources more than the guy I'm romantically involved with, it'll never work. At that point, he becomes a dependent and not a potential mate. This was exactly what happened with Brandon. I was fed up with our situation and he felt my frustration, which made him angry. I admit that I wasn't as mature as I should've been in dealing with him. My ego wouldn't allow him to think that he could just leave the situation. I knew he was used to dictating situations and calling the shots, but I was over it. Thus, I finally texted him and told him I thought we'd make better friends. And this was true. The night before I texted him, he came to my house uninvited and assumed that we would be intimate. Needless to say, I wasn't interested. His scent, which I once loved, lingered throughout my house after he'd left and it drove me crazy. I headed straight to the laundry mat the following morning to rid my things of his scent. It was awful. Pheromones are real and I didn't realize their impact on attraction until that moment.

I take full responsibility for my role in the fallout. I should've framed our relationship as "friends only" much sooner. I led him to believe that I cared more than I did even after he expressed his displeasure that things weren't progressing between us. But the truth is, I'm glad that I chose me. Being around him was suffocating, and I spent two to three weeks agonizing over what I should do about our situation and when to call it quits. I don't like hurting people and I never want to look like the bad person. However, being with him was no longer enjoyable. I didn't want to be anywhere near him. He didn't need to call me on the phone or text me. I was okay.

At some point, I stopped returning his calls and, if I happened to speak with him, I'd rush him off the phone. He still didn't get it. I'd always thought that once someone stopped making contact, they were no longer interested. He didn't get that message. I eventually had to put on my big girl underpants and

Notes: _____

_____

_____

_____

_____

directly let him know that it was over. At the end of the day, it wasn't fair to lead him on and have him thinking that we were moving in a positive direction. I gave him the opportunity to lead and be the man in my life, and I learned a lot from that experience. Ultimately, I chose to end things because that's what was best for *me*.

Our knowledge of dating comes from a number of sources — whether or not we had a man in the house growing up; the kind of relationship we've had (or haven't had) with our fathers; and what we learned through the media all shape our views about dating. Tanesha explains the kind of messages she received: "*I would say I received the wrong messages. I think I just realized this. Growing up without a father in the home, I sought out a father figure in the men I dated. I had the mindset that I wanted (not needed) a man to take care of me. It wasn't until I was on my own, taking care of myself, that I realized I'm able to take care of myself and love myself. [In hindsight], I would've had less 'relations' [and been more selective] with some of the people I was involved with. Your body really is your temple and everyone is not deserving of an entry pass.*"

Too often, black girls are left to figure out relationships on their own or rely on information from their peer group. Parents and guardians of black girls frequently warn them of what *not* to do, but that's only half of the message. What exactly *should* black girls do when it comes to romantic relationships? Ebony reflects on the messages she received from her family: *"I never had any conversations with my family about sex aside from the general 'don't do this' type stuff that's said in passing. My mother was a young mom. My aunts were married with children. I had a really close relationship with my grandmother who I called 'mom.' Because of this, I also had close relationships with my great aunts, my grandmother's sisters. I believe that my exposure to this older generation and their marriages gave me a different view on relationships. The people of my generation that I was around didn't seem to value relationships and what it meant to give yourself only to those who deserve you. I've had my share of experiences, but I'm glad to say that I've found myself and I understand the importance of sex, and how it's not just physical but spiritual, as well. For that reason, I cherish me."*

Notes: _____
_____
_____
_____

Choosing Us: Marriage

Relationships, we all want them. What many black women fail to realize, myself included, is that romantic relationships are necessary. We're creatures who are created for companionship. Through evolution and distorted socialization, however, the need for companionship has become a neurotic game of cat and mouse, which often leads to negative stereotypes about black women. Some of the stereotypes that are attributed to black women in relationships include: we are gold-diggers, argumentative, unappreciative, combative among other unsavory attributes. Despite our superhuman abilities, black women *are* human and we have the same needs as women in other ethnic groups.
The side effects of slavery, Jim Crow, the crack cocaine epidemic and mass incarceration has led to the deterioration of the black family unit, and has pitted black women against black men. The discord has been

Notes: _____

_____

_____

_____

unproductive and detrimental to the black community as a whole. I've witnessed enough of these "black women versus black men" relationship discussions and try my best to steer clear of them. The only point that I'd like to make — that I'm confident most black women will agree with — is that black women still WANT and NEED black men. Despite what broader society would have you think, black women desire for black men to step into the role of leaders. We don't want to do this alone. We believe in our black men and we're prepared to support them should their foundation shift. Black women are the cheerleaders for black men, not their opposition.

The beauty about the black woman is her ability to forgive and extend compassion even after her heart's been violated and trampled over numerous times. CeCe is a great example of finding the courage to trust, love and accept love: "*My dad was a deadbeat. This guy couldn't stay out of jail for two years straight. As a summation of drug use, robberies and poor decision making, he couldn't manage to live life on the outside. This created a perspective of inconsistency and sabotage, and ruined my ability to trust people, especially men. I was molested by a family friend. This deteriorated my trust for people. I didn't even trust my family enough to believe me. I didn't tell my story until I was out of college. This, coupled with insecurities, created a huge barrier between me and men. Intimacy was traumatizing."*

Despite being robbed of the opportunity to have a strong male presence early in her life, CeCe maintained her optimism on the possibility of love and healthy relationships. And, fortunately, she was able to heal past her trauma. CeCe gushes: *"I'm getting married! I finally allowed someone to get close enough to me to infiltrate my heart."*

I have very few friends that are married. LaToya is who I call one of the "lucky ones." She and her husband have been married for nearly 10 years and while things haven't always been great, they've manage to remain committed to each other. LaToya and I frequently discuss relationships and marriage. Though not an original contributor LaToya had a wealth of knowledge to share about marriage. According to LaToya, she and her husband had to learn about themselves individually and in their partnership. Once

Notes: _____

_____

_____

_____

_____

they were able to hit their stride while raising two sons, their marriage began to flourish abundantly. LaToya credits the success of her marriage to her and her husband defining their marriage for themselves and not allowing their family to participate in the dynamics of their marriage.

I think we can all agree there's no particular recipe for marriage. Sometimes people get it right and sometimes they don't. We absorb all that we've been exposed to regarding relationships, consider our personal preferences and simply pray for the best. Latisha reflects on her views about marriage: *"This is such a sensitive topic. Growing up, my parents fought and argued most of the time. My paternal grandparents 'tolerated' each other. My grandfather worked and my grandmother made sure to have his dinner ready when he came home from work. Neither couple displayed genuine affection and they often riled one another. When my grandmother fell ill, I remember my grandfather breaking down and telling me, 'I wouldn't want to do without her!'*

I had to unlearn what I witnessed about relationships during my upbringing. The only healthy relationship in my family is an aunt and uncle and they've been married for about 50 years. Relationships that didn't survive within my circle of friends and family sadden me. The older I get, the more I appreciate my husband because he's so supportive and doesn't subscribe to society's superficial expectations of a husband and wife. I feel these expectations are some of the problem with my friends' and family members' failed relationships. The biggest lesson I've learned is the importance of each person expressing gratitude and appreciation for their partner's tangible and intangible contributions to the marriage."

I've grown to appreciate marriage and all that it can be — giving and receiving selflessly, as well as learning and growing. Fruitful marriages aren't mythological. They do exist. They require love, selflessness and dedication. I grew up believing that I didn't need a man for anything because that was the message preached to me by the network of single mothers who cultivated me. Truth is, I *do* need a husband and I'm not ashamed to say so. This doesn't mean that I'll accept just *any* man in order to say that I have a husband. It means that I need someone who's

Notes: _____

_____

_____

_____

_____

willing to be my partner and companion, and who's willing to grow through life together. Ultimately, we must be honest about our wants and needs and, more importantly, unashamed to say them out loud.

WORKING WOMAN

Unfair Advantage

    Heaven forbid that a black woman does all the right things in the right manner and surpasses the competition. If a black woman does achieve such feat, it's often viewed as her somehow having an unfair advantage. Never mind when the deck is stacked against her using unjust and unethical rules that seemingly change as soon as each is identified and mastered. Black women aren't asking for favoritism or a savior; we're simply asking for the needle to not move every time we're close to achieving something great. We're asking the dominant power structure to stop making things more complicated than it needs to be. Black women learn the rules and play the game, but once we start winning, new rules are inserted as obstacles like a house game of Uno or Monopoly.

    In today's professional landscape, employability requires a college degree and, honestly, that oftentimes isn't enough. For the many black women who've

Notes: _____

_____

_____

_____

_____

matriculated or are currently working on their degree, many will tell you that it was no easy task. Jessica reflects on what she considers one of her top accomplishments: *"Graduating from college was a pivotal time in my life. I was the first generation to attend college with limited guidance. During this time, my grandfather passed away, my paternal grandmother was diagnosed with breast cancer, my parents divorced and my finances were bad. I went through a lot to walk across that stage. It taught me that I'm stronger than my circumstances. It also changed what I wanted from life. I'm definitely more conscious, as well."*

Many black women are the head of their household or the primary breadwinners – for whatever reason – and raising a family while maintaining a career may seem impossible. Tanesha discusses the challenge of having work-life balance: *"I think I always knew school and a career were important. Growing up in the projects, I wanted more for myself. So I placed the burden on myself. I still ascribe to it because I believe if you work hard and focus, you'll be successful. My biggest challenge is being a mother and a career woman. I'd love nothing more than to stay home and raise my kids, prepare fancy dinners and help with* homework. I'd also love nothing more than to take over the world. I find that both things conflict with each other. I want to be a 'BOSS' so to speak, but in doing so, what am I taking away from my kids? Both are equally important to me, so I walk a fine line of figuring out what needs my attention and when. I know that I'm not alone in feeling this way, but I also see my predicament as a problem that mothers face while dads don't. It's a part of being a working woman".

Black women are no strangers to hard work. We're taught early on that to succeed professionally, we must outwork our competition and understand that said work may not ever receive recognition. We learn from examples that include our parents, grandparents or extended family members, who often carried the proverbial stones that others received credit for. Ebony shares her experience with the examples she's had in her life: "*My grandmother would work throughout the night, and then come home to care for the family. She cooked dinner every day and worked every night. She worked in a factory making towels and*

Notes: _____

_____

_____

_____

_____

comforters. My dad did the same. My grandfather was in the military. He was honorably discharged. During this time, the schools were segregated in the small town we called home. They told me stories about how, despite the weather, they had to walk miles to and from school. My grandmother graduated high school, but my dad didn't. My mom finished high school as an adult and completed an associate's degree. My mom had me when she was 16-years-old. I have an older sister who's 1-1/2 years older than me. I also have two younger sisters. I believe my work ethic comes from my grandmother and my dad. We struggled a lot just to make ends meet. We never went without, which I attribute to my grandmother's determination to make ends meet. My family's struggles are what pushed me to where I am today and the reason I want to create a legacy for my own family. My family currently doesn't have a legacy to leave for future generations. I'm a first-generation college graduate who's currently pursuing my master's degree. I desire to start my own business so that I can create opportunities for others who share similar experiences and have a strong desire and work ethic to create change."

Positions of Power

There are members of society who'd rather not see black women in positions of power. In December 2017, Ed Lee, then-mayor of San Francisco, unexpectedly died of a heart attack. This resulted in London Breed, then-president of the San Francisco Board of Supervisors, serving as interim mayor. Breed is a San Francisco native from the historically-known Fillmore District, which later became the Western Addition area for transplants who've migrated. I consider London Breed to be among the women who overcame a troubling childhood to reach success. Breed is also a black woman. Needless to say, a shit storm erupted after Breed was named as Lee's successor. To summarize it politely: several of Breed's white American male colleagues refused to accept her new role because it placed her, as a black woman, in a position of power that was higher than theirs. And many of them made it clear, in no uncertain terms,

Notes: _____

_____

_____

_____

_____

that they wouldn't take orders from to a black woman. This might sound oversimplified, but it's the truth. Several local officials immediately sought ways to unseat Breed. As such, rules and policies that weren't implemented in the past or during Lee's tenure were suddenly necessary for Breed. The use of these optional rules appeared targeted as local leaders adamantly tried to enforce them. For many of San Francisco's constituents, it was hard not to assume that Breed faced the additional opposition because she's a Black woman.

  Despite the numerous attempts to discredit or invalidate her, Breed was the consummate professional. Perhaps there were moments where she went off within her highly-trusted inner circle, but publicly, she took the punches in stride, avoided negativity and performed the functions of her job. About a month after Breed assumed the interim mayor role, six board members elected to have her removed and requested that a "caretaker" mayor hold the seat until the special election was held in June 2018. According to the board members, they didn't want Breed listed as the incumbent on the special election ballot and wanted the mayoral race to be on an "even playing field." I call bullshit, but that's just me.

However, what others intend to harm you with, the Lord will use to build you up. Breed handled all of her challenges with dignity and grace. Breed is an excellent example of a black woman defying the odds and she now serves as the 45th mayor of the City and County of San Francisco.

In a world that sees our blackness and womanhood as a threat, how are black women supposed to excel in our careers? Tanesha is in an industry that's turning the tide on inclusivity and she reflects on her experiences: *"[I feel as though I'm] navigating a white world in a black woman's body. I work in an industry where it's predominately white men. There are very few women and even fewer people of color (POC). When I can, I try to always hire a woman or a POC because I want my workplace to be a melting pot and because growing up, I felt certain careers weren't an option for me. Everyone tells you to be a doctor or lawyer but no one says be a director or producer. And even if they do, you have to be exposed to [the industry]. I want to expose POC to everything*

Notes: _____
_____
_____
_____
_____

that I wasn't and give the youth as many options as possible so they can have a successful career."

Entrepreneurship is a door that can open to anyone who's interested in the opportunity to create, lead and be their own boss. CeCe maintains employment and has entered the world of entrepreneurship: *"Currently, I work with a nonprofit organization that provides emergency relief, educational sponsorship and basic needs to widows and orphans abroad. I also assist homeless teens with transitioning from homelessness to self-sufficiency. To add to the fun, I run a small online boutique, as well."*

We're currently in a space where black women are leaving the traditional career paths toward economic and professional growth to pursue their own business ventures. We're creating spaces where we feel comfortable and able to thrive, along with nurturing those who look like us. It's not uncommon to meet a black woman who owns her own business, but is also respectfully climbing the corporate ladder or soaring in her career field. If there's a path to professional success, black women will either find it or create it.

Stand Your Ground

Stand your ground. There are laws built around this concept. Yet, when it comes to employment and our economic needs, black women are especially likely to yield to the expectations or desires of others. If I've learned anything in the past three years, it's to be firm about what's right and what's fair for me. Consequently, my income hasn't been stable. In 2016 I separated from a job that was considered prestigious by my peers. And, though I was the Director of my own department for a San Francisco non-profit organization the experience was less than glamorous. Separating from this organization afforded me the opportunity to explore freelance work and consulting. Still, God is faithful because my bills remained paid – albeit sometimes late, but they still got paid.

In an effort to switch industries, I accepted a contract position with the goal of attaining a permanent position within six months. To my surprise,

Notes: _____

_____

_____

_____

_____

an even better position opened up that would yield more experience. My boss, who appreciated my productivity, recommended me as a candidate for senior management to consider.

Opportunities come to those who prepare. Be that as it may, not all opportunities are worthwhile. Unfortunately, the company's compensation scale was significantly below market based on the company's financial health. Since I was switching industries and entering a new marketplace, I was willing to play in the sand at a rate slightly below market due to my "inexperience," but not a significantly lower rate because the company simply couldn't afford to pay me. That wasn't my responsibility. When I show up and perform my duties, I expect to be compensated appropriately.

After a week of conversing with management about the role it was time to discuss compensation. As I predicted, management tried to sweet talk me into an insanely low salary. We couldn't agree on the 401(k) salary gap and I started to feel undervalued. Companies risk hiring lower quality candidates by not providing a decent and fair salary commensurate with the cost-of-living expenses. For the first time, I negotiated my salary. My boss supported me 100%

and he recognized that I simply wanted to be compensated fairly. Apparently, everyone working for that company was underpaid. During the final meeting, I was told, "Now is not a good time." Was I disappointed? Yes, I was interested and the position was a great opportunity. But for $5,000 less per year, I could do my current job with less stress. Thus, I declined the position. I really don't think I declined the job since the terms weren't right for me, but I stood my ground!

As a black woman, it's not always easy to stand firm on fair compensation. The ability to walk away is a liberty that not all black women have, and I didn't recognize the privilege in that until I actually walked away. There are too many variables at risk. Still, I was committed to standing my ground so that whatever the outcome, I knew God had it all in His hands. I didn't have a care in the world when it came to making the decision. I made an informed and fair decision that wasn't contingent upon any external variables. My finances shouldn't influence my ability to accept what

Notes: _____
_____
_____
_____
_____

is right and fair.

I was proud of myself. I stepped into one of the largest arenas of my professional life and I came to the bargaining table with a clear head and sound heart. I was unafraid. I wasn't intimidated. It was my truth versus the company's needs. The company doesn't need me that much if it wasn't willing to come to a meeting point. I walked out the room. I advocated for myself. I was fair to both myself and the company. Ultimately, the more prestigious position wasn't the best option for me. The cost of doing business with me has gone up and it's time that I inform my business associates. It's time to stop shortchanging myself and pursue what God has called me to do.

There are numerous social, economic and institutional reasons why black women sometimes lag behind their peers. It's certainly not for a lack of trying. More frequently, black girls and women are more intentional with their time and talents because they know they can't afford to be mediocre. Jessica shares her experience and observation with the passion versus purpose dichotomy: *"I feel like most black parents tell their children to go college [in order] to be successful. Not many teach them about being their own boss and creating generational wealth. I was told that I HAD to go to college. Despite having a love for the arts and not having a clear vision for my future, I went to college as I was expected to. From the experience, I learned so much and I'm grateful. But I'm more grateful that it doesn't define me or my happiness. I've learned that having a purpose matters more than having material things. I hope to someday have children and help them find their purpose rather than a career. I'll teach them to not to conform to what society says success is. But rather, do whatever makes them happy."*

In many black households, education is strongly encouraged, if not required. While these values are taught, not all parents and caregivers have the ability to offer black students the support that they need in order to be successful. Latisha shares her unique academic journey: *"Growing up, my family never talked about the expectation of going to college. My mother only had an eighth grade education and became a parent in her early teens. By the time she was 22, she was the mother of five children. My mother worked at*

Notes: _____
_____
_____
_____
_____

the same restaurant for 30 years. She practically helped build the restaurant through her commitment to doing her best and providing great customer service, even though the pay was just above a livable wage. My father attended community college for a short time. I remember my classmates discussing plans to attend a particular college when I was in high school, but at the time, my siblings and I were separated from my parents. Because I had missed a number of days during my junior year, I was in jeopardy of failing the 11th grade. It was difficult for me to focus at any level. Because I'd experienced so much adversity, the district decided to hire a tutor to come to my group home and get me caught up. In the 12th grade, I was on schedule to graduate, but I struggled. I remember the sigh of relief I gave when I found out I had enough credits to graduate. At the age of 28, I graduated with a degree in information systems. My husband is also a college graduate. We've always instilled the importance of education in our children. They attended private schools for the majority of their early education because we felt the early investment was important and necessary. Because of our previous struggles, my husband and I are compassionate and empathetic people. Even with our parenting, our children know that what matters *most is 'how you show up' for yourself at school, during an interview, at the workplace or wherever you are. It makes a difference when you do good work."*

Notes: _____
_____
_____
_____
_____

FINDING PEACE

Stress Management

Stress will literally kill you. And I haven't found a person on God's green earth who's faced with more stressors than the black woman. We're naturally concerned about our community, our children, our men, our families and our economic needs because we usually bear most of the responsibility in these areas. Notice that I intentionally omitted concerns for black women's physical and mental health because this is an area where most of us fall short. Black women have passed on the spirit of personal neglect for generations. Only recently have we become comfortable with expressing our feelings of stress without apologizing for it. Because black women are prone to showing up, getting things done and suppressing our emotions, the world erroneously believes that we don't have stress. This couldn't be further from the truth.

It's true, we do execute. Rather, we get shit done

Notes: _____
_____
_____
_____
_____

because if we don't, who else has the skill and competency to do it? This mindset is often ingrained in us. Though it's an asset in most environments, it's detrimental to our psyche and physical health. More than ever before, it's necessary for black women to take on a self-care approach. The task isn't easy and, for some, it's uncomfortable but we need to invest in ourselves. The most important thing I learned about managing my stress was that if I became incapacitated, the entity I was killing myself for would simply replace me. For the company, it'd be just another body to occupy the space I once had and my contributions may or may not receive recognition.

In short, I had to become comfortable with setting boundaries. I also had to remind myself that I couldn't allow some outside entity that I had no control over to kill me. Period! There's so much life to live and sickness or the preoccupation of stress is counterproductive to sharing your gifts with the world. It's important to dial into yourself, recognize your stressors and learn how to respond to them. Recognizing your stressors allows you the opportunity to learn how to do things differently to avoid repeating those negative experiences.

As we mature, how we view the world and how we interact with it changes. Tanesha rediscovered the importance of religion in her life and shares how she navigates through the current climate: *"Religion plays somewhat of a role in my life. I grew up Baptist but as a teenager, I shied away from the church. As an adult, I've attended Bible studies in an effort to understand and draw closer to God. I previously held the opinion that people only draw near to God when they're in need but now I know better. Sometimes, you just want to say, 'Thank you' or you need someone to talk to and God can be that person for you. He may not answer how you want but He does answer. I would like to devote more time to my studies. I want to have a better understanding of the Bible and becoming a better person. I think those things will only happen once I open myself up more to God. With my new studies, I feel as if a lot of people are misled. I feel that people should read the Bible for themselves and not take the word of others. The Bible says, 'Love thy neighbor.' I think this is forgotten and ignored. We're all God's*

Notes: _____

_____

_____

_____

_____

people. President Trump wants to build a wall to keep out the 'bad hombres' but if he were a true Christian, he would do more to help rather than hurt."

Rejection is Hard

I've lived my entire life as one big contradiction: pursue success but avoid rejection. Rejection is unavoidable on the road to success. Perhaps that's why I'm not as successful as I imagined I'd be. Although I know I rejection is inevitable, my introduction to the catastrophic phenomenon has stagnated both my personal and professional life. The rejection I felt from my father's absence still haunts me and it'll continue to do so until I do the necessary work and repair what was broken. This doesn't require my dad's presence or his permission.

I probably wouldn't feel as rejected if I never heard from my father after he left when I was three-years-old. However, I grew up with a telephone father. My father was a church deacon and in an attempt to uphold his "good Christian" image, he upheld the bare minimum when it came to communicating with his children. I'd come to expect the occasional phone calls

Notes: _____

_____

_____

_____

and birthday cards throughout my childhood and into adulthood. Truthfully, if I didn't make the effort to reach out to my father, I would've never met him or his side of the family. To feel rejected by my father is a hurt that I can't begin to describe. It has significantly altered my life and, thus, my behavior in ways that I couldn't recognize until now.

    I doubt that my father even recognizes how his absence and behavior has caused rejection. He's a product of his own environment since, to some degree, his father rejected him. The subconscious mind is a tricky place. It's not surprising that my father hasn't been able to break the cycle. In an effort to gain a better understanding of myself, I started recognizing certain patterns and challenging myself to overcome them. As a result, I avoid situations in both professional and romantic environments that may result in me experiencing feelings of rejection. Romantically, I avoid rejection from men like the plague. Instead of taking a chance on love and exploring the depth that it has to offer, I tend to cut things short before the situation gets too deep or he changes his mind about me. If my father left, why wouldn't a guy that I'm dating not do the same? So, I leave him before he has the chance to leave me. I need to change this.

I'm aware that this thought process is counterintuitive to my goals. In processing my feelings of rejection, I've had to learn that what others do has nothing to do with me. In fact, rejection is oftentimes God's redirection. God redirects me onto the path that He wants for me. Therefore, I don't need to take things so personal. I must learn to find peace with the absence of something I once held in high regard. Being rejected doesn't mean I wasn't "good enough." It means the opportunity (or person) wasn't for me at a particular time, and that there's something greater on the horizon. Experiencing rejection hurts, and it's colored how I interacted in the world. What was once a coping a mechanism to avoid rejection turned into a cage that prevented me from spreading my wings. I want to fly. I need to fly. I have to fly. I'm prepared to do what it takes to no longer allow rejection to be my warden. I can't replace what causes the feelings of rejection but I can learn how to better deal with it.

Notes: _____
_____
_____
_____
_____

Rejection takes on many forms and impacts us differently from social exclusion to self-sabotage. Jessica shares her journey toward self-acceptance: *"Navigating the world in a fat body is very challenging. It's hard to practice self-love and self-care when you're constantly reminded that your body isn't acceptable. I've had highs and lows with self-acceptance. There were times when I practiced body positivity and times when I obsessed about changing myself. Body image influences your life choices like dating, socializing and even careers. I struggled in all aspects. Time has taught me that the people who criticize others' bodies under the guise of health concerns are truly driven by vanity. Therefore, I don't need to absorb that energy. Mental health is key in making healthy decisions. I've started working on that and it's made a difference in how I live day-to-day.*

My parents' divorce changed how I viewed marriage and men. I'm not fond of change and seeing a man that I've known since I was 4-years-old go through change was emotionally draining for me. It took a toll on all of us emotionally and financially. I'm still very guarded. Trust is also something I struggled with due to so many people walking away or turning a blind eye during my most vulnerable time."

As children, most of the events that occur are beyond our control. Children have to rely on adults for leadership, guidance and care. If a child's foundation becomes unstable via trauma, it'll impact the manner in which that child views the world. Latisha discusses how she overcame her childhood experiences: *"At the age of 10, I had the opportunity to visit my paternal grandmother in California and I lived there until I was 13. While in California, I learned there was trouble at home and my sisters were removed from the home. My eldest brother was forced to leave at 16, but I can't remember the circumstances. There were accusations of incest committed by my father. I returned home and, shortly thereafter, things started to unravel. My father started abusing me and I became another victim. My mom finally moved out and got her own place. After that, my dad moved his long-time girlfriend into our home. We had a disagreement and he kicked me out the house. I was 16 and pregnant when I was placed in a group home, but had to abort the pregnancy because an ultrasound detected an abnormality in the baby's heart.*

Notes: _____

_____

_____

_____

_____

I stayed in the foster care system until I aged out at 18-years-old. By that time, my five siblings and I were either living in a group home, foster care or as an independent minor.

From my experience, I learned that family dynamics can have lasting implications. My spirit was dismantled and my energy was depleted over time because standing in my truth and telling the truth had consequences. It was like going to battle with the people who were supposed to support and care for me. Instead, I was shunned because I wouldn't let things go. I continuously reminded people of who my father was [and what he'd done] and I was often chastised or told to 'leave it alone.' Eventually, I made the decision to remove myself from the chaos and, essentially, divorce every member of my family whose energy no longer served me. The biggest challenge is healing my childhood trauma and understanding how that showed up in my adult life. It continues to be a struggle."

Additionally, feeling excluded or misjudged by society also causes feelings of rejection. Black women are constantly fed images through the media that tell us we're not valuable, desirable or simply good enough. CeCe shares how she built the emotional muscle to accept her beauty: *"I was black and fat.*

Well, I'm still black and fat but my perspective is different. Compared to my cousins, I was the darkest and the heaviest! I still am! I was called 'ugly' and 'Miss Celie' from The Color Purple, and bullied by boys. I was silently depressed. I thought the world hated me. I thought I was plagued with darkness. I also felt like the world hated my dark skin. I felt that it made me inferior. I also compared my beauty to an industrial standard of beauty."

Rejection from any family members is hurtful, but it's especially painful when the rejection comes from someone who's tasked with your daily care. Ebony reflects on how her physical appearance impacted her familial relationships: *"Being a light-skinned woman or, as my family would say, 'a dirty red,' I was always treated differently. Different wasn't always good. I was the outcast most of the time by those who meant the most to me. I was left out of family sleepovers and called names like 'sidewalk baby' because of something I had no control over. I was given this name because I was raised by my grandmother*

Notes: _____
_____
_____
_____
_____

and either not wanted by my mom or taken from her depending on whose side of the story I believed. I didn't meet my mom until I was about 12-years-old when she bought me a Barbie doll from Family Dollar for my birthday. After that, I saw her once a year until about 15 or 16-years-old.

At 16, I moved in with my mom because I was experiencing abuse from my dad and other family members. My dad was on drugs REALLY bad. He would get paid on Friday and was broke by Saturday. My aunt, who was my protector, would fuss and argue with him just so I could have the things that I needed for school or for Christmas. When my aunt passed, Christmas did, too. I was an excellent student academically. Behaviorally, I was a monster. I acted up in school. I got paddled on a regular basis. That's right, the school principal would use a wooden paddle right on my backside. I was so familiar with the paddle that I automatically knew the position. It became a routine. However, no one [at school] knew what I was feeling inside. Inside, I was angry from feeling rejected by my mom and my family. It was pretty hard, at least in my eyes."

Feelings of rejection are often magnified when our perceived rejection comes from God, our source of life. Growing up in the church, CeCe had a unique perception of the world, the church and what was expected of her: "[It was all about] *Jesus, Jesus, Jesus, Jesus! Growing up as a preacher's kid wasn't easy. I was forced to believe [in God]. I was forced to go to church. I was forced to participate in worship. Because of this, I slightly resented the church. I believe it deprived me of my childhood. Conversely, it also birthed a hunger for faith and spiritual enlightenment. Faith is integrated into my being, but my perspective of faith, church and spiritual appropriation is changing. As a result of my growth in faith, I have a more progressive view of religion. I'm more focused on living a more balanced life. I was afraid to enjoy life because I feared going to hell. I was taught that everything that was 'fun' had a hellacious intention. THANK JESUS FOR CHANGE!"*

Notes: _____

_____

_____

_____

Superwoman

Somewhere between metallic glass and a diamond lies the strength of a black woman. The question is *why*? Why are black women expected to be exceptionally strong and carry the burdens of others? Heaven forbid that a black woman falls short of society's expectations of her super strength because then, she's called everything but a child of God.

It's hard to find a black woman who hasn't felt completely responsible for everything occurring in her life at some point. And while experiencing this, she likely felt that she didn't have the time or space to crack or crumble under the pressure. Growing up, I couldn't make any excuses. I was simply encouraged to "do what you gotta' do." This may sound like sage advice, but in highly stressful situations where the ultimate goal was survival, this method had short-term benefits with long-term consequences. In doing whatever I had to do, I didn't have the opportunity to

Notes: _____

_____

_____

_____

critically assess a situation and make the best decision. I only did what was needed to get through the present moment.

I'm not alone in this line of thinking. This philosophy has trickled down from generation to generation of black women. Historically, black women were omitted from institutional, cultural and interpersonal discussions surrounding mental health. Only recently has the conversation started about the importance of black women's emotional and mental health, and how a deficit in these areas impacts our daily lives and the decisions we make. Even within the black community, mental illness and mental health are treated as taboo topics. Research is limited regarding how mental illness specifically manifests in black people compared to the highly-researched, baseline group of white Americans.

During undergrad, I visited my psychology professor during office hours and she shared with me that people study psychology to discover and learn more about themselves. Back then, I dismissed the idea, but it wasn't until I completed my master's program in clinical psychology, that her words rang true. I lived most of my life in survival mode — going nonstop like the Energizer Bunny and unfocused with my time and talents.

As someone who's older, wiser and more patient (with myself and my immediate world), I'm more cognizant of my being, learning who I am and aware that I'm evolving. Needless to say, my beloved professor was right. Earning two degrees in psychology required me to work through my trauma and baggage. Most black women don't have the formal training or exposure to identify their pain and trauma. We started creating spaces for black women to convene and share, but it's not nearly at the rate the trauma was inflicted. Still, those gains are necessary no matter how slowly they come.

I'd like to consider Jessica's journey for a moment: *"My grandfather joked that I was really his baby because he paid the hospital bill. Not too long after* [we moved from Mississippi to Massachusetts], *my mom met my stepfather, moved to Lowell, Massachusetts, and had four more children. As the oldest, I learned responsibility despite living a middle-*

Notes: _____
_____
_____
_____

class lifestyle. After 15 years of marriage, my parents divorced. That same year, my grandfather died. Those events solidified a bond between my siblings and me that can't be explained. Because everything around us was crumbling, we knew all we had was each other. Things became tough financially and we really struggled. Losing our patriarch (my grandfather) really caused a shift in my extended family. The love has changed but we continue to show up despite that. Fortunately, I'm blessed with an abundance of love from my mom, siblings and friends."

Sexual assault: "A male friend manipulated a situation, and for some time, I blamed myself for being there and allowing it to happen. After it happened, I forced myself to hang around him to soothe his guilt despite feeling uncomfortable simply because he said he was sorry. It ruined my self-esteem. My self-care diminished. I gained more weight. I isolated myself. I grew very distrustful of men. Another man I trusted, also hurt me. I felt like I couldn't tell anyone because I didn't want anyone judging me. So I suffered silently like many women do."

Experiencing loss: "Losing someone is never easy. And I've had the misfortune of experiencing loss one too many times. I lost my grandfather, paternal *grandmother, three great aunts, one aunt, one uncle and three cousins. Each death affected me deeply. There isn't one loss that I didn't struggle with. I used self-medicating to soothe my depression. One of the most challenging losses was my cousin, Jasmine. We were very close. She was one of the few family members on my father's side that I knew very well. I never imagined losing her so young. It was definitely a hard pill to swallow. The depression I went through was very intense, but through God's grace, I'm still standing. It's taught me how precious life is. I also learned the power of forgiveness. I'm working on establishing a relationship with my father now that I'm an adult. I'm processing things differently now. The world will never be the same place. That's why I want to try to help others heal. Because I know what it's like to feel broken and alone."*

Being a black woman and "super" doesn't mean we have to go through life abused and unhealed. We increase our power when we acknowledge the bad things that have occurred and take the necessary time

Notes: _____

_____

_____

_____

_____

to heal. Latisha gives us insight to her life in a family where the women were all superwomen and what they sacrificed for such a title: *"Growing up in a family where there was much trauma and adversity, I became desensitized to expressing feelings and emotions. Nurturing my children was a challenge because my parents' objective was raising children, not nurturing them. I can't recall my mother telling me, 'I love you' or showing affection until I became an adult. As an adult, emotions became layered and complicated over time because there were unreconciled, raw emotions from what I'd experienced. The responsibilities of parenting and marriage, as well as family dynamics started to manifest and life seemed out-of-control most of the time. There were stages in my life where I felt depleted and emotionally drained because I felt things were falling through the cracks all the time and I was spread thin. It's important for me to stress that being resilient has its limitations. As black women, we've been taught that in order to be strong, we must take on whatever comes our way.*

I recently had a conversation with my mother about her relationships and I realized that my mother had to physically and emotionally fight for respect all of her life. Even with her 8th grade education, she managed to buy a home and maneuver through a bureaucratic system to have her home repaired when it was damaged by fire. I say this because, oftentimes, I find myself looking for answers in books, people and workshops. I've only recently begun to appreciate the life lessons received through my mother's and my siblings' resilience.

As an incest survivor, my development was abruptly interrupted by a suppressed rage and I resented my misfortune. That feeling was alive, but dormant and I lived life in the shadow of a secret. I camouflaged my hurt with the biggest smile that I could muster. People would often notice and comment on how happy I was, but in contrast, the smile veiled the scars of a broken spirit. The most challenging hurdle I overcame was the subconscious war that I'd declared on myself. I knew I was a strong person, but being around family tested and sometimes frayed that strength. Consequently, I was often chastised for my mouth despite telling the truth. Oftentimes, I would hold my breath and tongue to keep the peace when I felt that

Notes: _____

_____

_____

_____

_____

the conversations with my family were disingenuous and formulated.

In my late 20s, I made an agreement with myself that I'd bind my internal rage and declared, 'enough is enough!' It was time for me to start living for myself, knowing that the consequences might include betrayal, estrangement and backlash. When I started to speak my truth and name the pain and its perpetrator, relationships were tested. In the end, I stood alone with my sister and husband by my side. I learned that ignoring reality dismisses one's responsibility to take action, and that chaos is sometimes an addiction. My family used denial and disillusionment as smoke screens to block out reasoning. This prohibited them from hearing and me from speaking the truth. I had to remind myself that irrational behavior couldn't be rationalized and their attitudes and behaviors were, essentially, irrational. Walking away and refusing to look back was like walking on a bed of hot coals — it hurt, but reaching the other side was necessary for my healing. Family visits and telephone calls eventually ceased. Though I felt liberated, a tinge of confusion surfaced thereafter. I told the truth! Why do I feel as if my world is falling apart?

I grieved for my family, especially for my children because they were too young to understand the extremity of a situation that became volatile. Shortly after my decision to walk away, I experienced an unfamiliar shift, which catapulted into a subtle descent into depression. Life was pushing back when I wanted (and needed) to move beyond what was familiar. Depression was my voice of reason pulling me back to reconcile what I'd suppressed in order to function and survive. It wasn't something that I could 'get over.' Even when I felt like I was in control of my emotions, depression was an undercurrent waiting to surface whenever my emotions were ripe with inadequacy.

In my early 30s, a few years after the birth of my daughter, Adamma, depression began to take its toll and I realized that I needed help. After a one-time, 20-minute consultation with a psychiatrist, I left with a prescription for an antidepressant and mood stabilizer. After researching the side effects and associated costs, I decided to explore my options and possible alternatives before taking the medication. Let me

Notes: _____

_____

_____

_____

_____

reiterate that this was a personal decision. I'm neither discouraging nor encouraging the use of medication. I recommend that anyone facing mental health challenges seek counsel from a mental health professional. My decision not to use the prescribed medication resulted from my own journey of self-discovery. This wasn't a one-size-fits-all decision, but a personal choice to go in a different direction. I decided to define my own happiness by living my life with purpose. I knew that if I pushed back and made small attempts to name and address the source of my pain, my outlook on life would change, and it did. By redefining my own happiness through self-acceptance, I was able to release old habits of co-dependency, as well as thought patterns that negated my needs. I've completely engaged myself in the creative process, trusting that I'm mindfully acting out my purpose at this stage in my life."

    As black women, we often find ourselves being everything for everyone else except ourselves. This can lead to self-neglect. Our genuine care for others is a gift and a curse, a gift because people do need people to release and vent about stressors and misfortunes. Equally, it is a curse because the time we spend listening and supporting others is time not spent addressing our own issues. Ebony recounts her experiences of being a support system for others during her own time of needing emotional support: *"Aside from my tangible talents, I'm a people person. I develop relationships easily with others whether it's friendships, partnerships, work or school. As a result, people often come to me for advice or help when they're in need. It's truly a gift to have the ability to connect with other people and provide a word of encouragement despite what you may be feeling or dealing with on the inside. Many times, I found myself fighting back tears from [suppressing] my own troubles when someone came to me with a situation. You know what I'm talking about — that balled-up knot in your chest and throat that badly hurts from holding back the waterfalls, making your heart feel like it's about to explode. I've been there many times. Someone once said [to me], 'The strongest people make time to help others, even if they are struggling with their own problems.'"*

Notes: _____
_____
_____
_____
_____

BLACK.

WHITE.

SOCIETY.

Black by the Numbers

Black women aren't Captain Save-a-Society! We are overlooked and pushed aside until we're needed, and then we're expected to radically influence or shift the needle in a direction that likely doesn't benefit us. For two years, since the inauguration of the current president, white women have organized multi-city "women's marches" to protest the president and his maltreatment of women. There might've been other issues that these protesters sought to illuminate, but one thing is for certain, those issues had little to do with black women. How do I know? More often than not, I have observed white women in America seek "numbers" to support their grievances which includes roping in the influence and participation of black women. Truthfully, America's entire social structure is disadvantageous toward black women, and white women benefit from certain elements of this social structure. If nothing else, white privilege grants them

Notes: _____

_____

_____

_____

_____

access into arenas that black women are oftentimes unaware of. I'm not going to apologize for not supporting initiatives that don't have my best interest in mind as a black woman. So, no, I'm won't attend any women's march. Point me in the direction of the next black women's march, focusing on issues that specifically impact black women and I'll be there with bells on!

Let's take a moment to discuss the special election in Alabama in the latter part of 2017. The election was for the state senate seat left vacant by United States Attorney General Jeff Sessions. On the ballot were Doug Jones and Roy Moore, an accused child sex offender. The people of Alabama were in a conundrum: should they vote for the Democratic candidate who prosecuted the man responsible for bombing a black church and killing four black girls, or should they vote for the Republican candidate who was an accused sex offender? For the people that I associate with, the decision is a no-brainer. Most intelligent and morally sound people wouldn't want someone who's harmed children to serve as an elected official. As it turned out, election night results revealed that the significant turnout of black-women voters was the moral compass of that election. Alabama's constituents rejoiced and were praised for electing Doug Jones. Fake news! The white population of voters in Alabama *overwhelmingly* voted for Roy Moore. It was pretty disappointing to see the media attempt to issue a gold star to a segment of white America when it almost elected a pedophile. Black women were the true heroes of the election. Of course, I'm proud that black people have access to the democratic process of voting. However, it's unfortunate that black women's contribution to the process was immediately co-opted as "Alabamans did a great job." Let's be clear: black women saved Alabama's ass like we've done so many times before. Yet, they still didn't get the credit that was deserved. Because this repeatedly happens, black women usually don't allow such things to get them down. We learn to keep moving and we become more selective of where we exert our energy.

    The presence of black women ought to fill national news headline and social media timelines. We should be celebrated for our impact and how we improve every aspect of society that we encounter.

Notes: _____

_____

_____

_____

_____

Jessica shares: "*I want to be a blessing to everyone around me. I want to make people laugh. I want to continue to heal and love. I want my children to do the same.*" Tanesha adds: "*My daughter asked me what are my talents and I'm trying to figure that out. I want to be the best mom I can be and raise my two girls to know their worth. I think my supermom powers would be well-served.*"

Being a Black woman is exciting, beautiful and filled with contradiction. Latisha shares the legacy she wants to leave in the world: "*The legacy I want to be known for is creating beauty and telling my story. I think the long-term impact of childhood trauma is oftentimes overlooked and ignored, especially in black communities and families. Generational trauma is a wound we carry from one generation into the next. Pain isn't something that black people talk about because it's often misinterpreted or misunderstood. Family members often told me that the trauma that I experienced happened 'a long time ago' and I should 'get over it and move on.' Historically, this is what we've done with our pain. We erase it with denial and when it shows up, we punish ourselves and each other for '[not] acting right' [and ignoring our traumatic experiences]. I want the world to look at my art or read my prose and know that*

I created everything with intention. I communicate to myself and others that we're worthy of love and self-care in all of its healthy forms."

We cannot rest on the progress we've made thus far when there's so much more work ahead of us. CeCe shares her perspective on where black people are in America: *"We who believe in freedom cannot rest. As a community, we're doing a poor job at equipping our children in politics, community engagement and development. The political climate continues to decline and only work in the favor of the elite. I truly believe that we need to create more programs that teach our children the importance of community engagement and education."*

Notes: _____
_____
_____
_____

White People

The black American versus white American dichotomy will continue to draw a wedge in America until white Americans (as a whole) accept that black Americans are people too. We are not property (slavery ended in 1865) and we are not beasts that live in the wild that need containment. White Americans need to do more with shifting how they see and interact with black Americans. White Americans need to understand that whether black or white people have similar needs; food, safety and shelter, and want similar things, access to resources to live and raise healthy families. Perspective is everything. Some people live in the world and are unaware of who they are and how their presence impacts the spaces they walk into. Black women don't have this luxury. We're almost always aware of our environment and who's in it. We recognize that we can't arrive in a new space and be readily accepted for our authentic selves if we're in the

Notes: _____

_____

_____

_____

minority. Conversely, white people have the expectation of feeling free and comfortable in the world. Anything infringing upon that presumed right causes severe emotional and psychological distress. Black women simply call it Thursday or any other day of the week. Black women anticipate disturbances and work dubiously to overcome them. We're taught that focusing on barriers, challenges and setbacks only hinders us from achieving what otherwise could be done. We recognize that it's important to consider what should or could happen; however, it's more productive to focus on the now and "what is." To state it plainly, "shoulda', coulda', woulda' don't get you anywhere" as the popular phrase goes.

Self-love isn't taught, it's learned. Black women are taught to love and nurture others until they have nothing left for themselves. False doctrine! I learned that giving all I had to others left me empty. It was as if all of my resources were in a single bank and if someone needed something and I had it to give, I'd give it to them. Why? Because I was taught to help others by any means necessary. Today, wisdom and maturity has taught me to place my resources in separate accounts. I'm a lot more discerning with the resources that I allot for others.

Race relations in America will always be a hot topic of discussion until white people hold other white people accountable for their prejudicial behavior and actively call them out on such behavior in order to correct it. Jessica expresses her perspective on race relations: *"It's disturbing and discouraging. After all our ancestors have endured, we're still facing prejudice and injustice. What's most disheartening is witnessing others deny that racism exist while we have a racist president in office with thousands of his followers spewing hate. How blind can you be?"*

Being a black woman in our current sociopolitical climate is sometimes unbearable. We need spaces to speak to our truth and discuss our feelings. Tanesha shares her position on the current sociopolitical climate: *"I hate to say it, but, it's overwhelming. I should be focused on work and my kids, but [what's happening in our country] is all that I can focus on. Times have changed but, in some ways, things have remained the same. It sucks, but I feel that*

Notes: _____

_____

_____

_____

_____

in this life, things will never be perfect. That doesn't justify the current practices that are in place."

Latisha elaborates on how society's woes can impact black women's mental health: *"Mental health wellness is essential. As a community, we need more education to understand generational trauma and how it shows up, especially in our disciplinary practices. When we were disciplined with a belt as children, I believe that at times certain acts of whipping emitted a level of rage from the adults. I remember welts on my buttocks and my back. I remember lining up on my parents' bed in anticipation of a whipping or being summoned one at a time to find out 'who did it' when no one came forward. We were all punished. Those acts mimic the abuse of slavery. I believe that through microaggression and racism, black people are continuously experiencing the aftermath of slavery. Living in a society where we're not valued and denied our humanity, has taken a toll on our families and communities. We're experiencing a mental health crisis that no other race or ethnic group has had to systematically endure.*

We've stepped back in time! I feel the rise of our first black president resulted in an outcry of 'white fright' and a decline in civility, decency, humility and personal accountability. The current administration has been hijacked by a wannabe dictator and most of the key stakeholders in his administration have a credibility problem, which, in fact, has compromised the credibility of our country from a global standpoint. I remember Michael Moore was interviewed and he spoke about his greatest fear being a Trump Presidency and everything he spoke of has transpired. One would think it was a reality show, but this is real life and the most powerful man in the world is just a jackass.

As bell hooks defines it, this country is structured as a "white supremacist capitalist patriarchy" that only benefits the handful of billionaires who seem to want more than their billionaire neighbors. There are people in our society, especially those living in rural communities, who continuously vote against their own interest. I was watching television and a woman was asked a question about Obamacare and she responded that she didn't want Obamacare, she wanted the Affordable Care Act health plan. They're the same thing. President Obama left behind a thriving economy; however, wages haven't caught up with the rising cost

Notes: _____

_____
_____
_____
_____

of living. It's not unusual to hear that a person is holding down two or three jobs to cover the costs of their basic needs. Living in California, that's become the norm; hence, the surge in the "gig" economy. I've talked to Uber/Lyft drivers who have great jobs, but they still struggle to make ends meet.

The socioeconomic woes in recent years have changed the face of homelessness. You have skilled, employable and working individuals living in tent communities or in their vehicles. There are more individuals who're one paycheck or an illness away from becoming homeless and the safety nets are less available and accessible. Case in point, I made a constructive decision to quit my job in May [2018] and I applied for unemployment. My initial claim was denied so I appealed. I received a letter instructing me to reopen my claim. I called the Employment Development Department office almost daily for one month and never talked to one person. I recently attended my appeal hearing and I was approved for benefits three months later. Fortunately, in the meantime, we had savings and I was able to scale my art business to replace the loss of income. One thing I teach my daughter and try to show by example is discovering what you're passionate about and finding a way to monetize it. Some may call it a side hustle, side gig or hobby. Employment is not guaranteed, and over the years, workplace environments, benefits and loyalties have changed drastically because people are viewed as expendable."

Notes: _____
_____
_____
_____
_____

People of Color

"People of color" is not a justifiable categorization of non-whites. First, white isn't and shouldn't be the baseline. Second, clumping all non-whites into one category undermines the unique culture and experiences that each person has. Black people aren't people of color. We're people of significance, people of magic, or, more accurately, people of power. This is why our personhood is always under attack. Don't call or refer to me as a person of color. I find it rude and disrespectful.

What does it mean to be a person of color and how does that align with the overall goals for black people? Ebony shares her perspective: *"There's too much happening in society right now, which I feel has impacted the current thought processes and positions of black people. People are used as pawns to avoid the broader issues at hand. We're hunted down and killed just for simply being black. We're hated by people from*

Notes: _____
_____
_____
_____

all over the world just for being black. D.L. Hughley said it best, 'The worst place for a black person to be is in a white person's imagination.' White people — other races, too but white people in particular — don't think of black people as humans. They only see our skin color and what they want us to be. We've been stripped of everything from our history and we haven't been able to recover from it because they've maintained the authority to keep us oppressed and suppressed under their power. Under this current administration, we need to work in private to change ourselves and our mindsets while we create families and transcend those oppressive beliefs by working together within our community and only our community. We're a people who [values] family, closeness and traditions. We're warriors by nature. Royalty. What others think shouldn't define us. Instead, we define who we are."

BOWL, LID, SPOON

Grab a Plate

The women participating in this project reflect a snapshot of what many black women endure. For each story shared, there are millions more that are untold. What's true across the board for black women is that no matter the circumstances, we'll find a way to prevail. Our goal is to overcome obstacles in a healthier and more productive manner. We don't need to work ourselves to death. We don't have to neglect our needs. And we're no longer remaining silent. As we prepare our heads and hearts for future endeavors, the ladies have a final message for readers:

Be proud of your accomplishments. If you have worked hard for a goal that you set for yourself, acknowledge it. Jessica shares: *"[I'm most proud of] graduating high school and college, cleaning up my credit, buying my first car and overcoming depression. I was able to accomplish these things despite the circumstances surrounding them. Through all adversity,*

Notes: _____

_____

_____

_____

_____

I prevailed. They may seem like little things, but as a black woman coming from where I'm from, they matter to ME." Be curious about the world. Your primary environment is not the only place in the world, there is much you can learn and experience by interacting with others. Tanesha encourages us to: *"Try EVERYTHING, be more open and don't be afraid to be your own BOSS. Most importantly, TRAVEL, TRAVEL, TRAVEL."*

Be kind to yourself. Life is hard and despite what you have faced you are a survivor. Find a way to take care of your mental and emotional needs. Latisha shares*: "I know there's a miraculous higher power beyond what any man can understand or interpret. My premise for living is 'cause no harm' and the golden rule of 'do unto others as you have those do unto you.' I've used my creative talents to create stories of strength, resilience and reconciliation. I've exposed my pain by sharing my story in hopes that it helps others to heal from their spoken or unspoken pain."*

Be mindful of who you are and where you are. Life will forever have competing priorities, it's important that you make yourself priority number one. CeCe encourages us to: *"Do whatever sets your soul on fire! You will fail, but failure is the platform for future success. BE INTENTIONAL!"*

REFLECTIONS

REFLECTIONS

REFLECTIONS

REFLECTIONS

ABOUT THE AUTHOR

Nzinga D. Mpenda was born and raised in San Francisco, CA. Growing up in the city's Bayview Hunter's Point neighborhood shaped Nzinga's curiosity about people and their behavior. Through her own challenging childhood experiences Nzinga fosters empathy for those who are products of impoverished upbringings. Nzinga credits the diversity of San Francisco for recognizing the range in people and herself.

Human connection and commitment to growth is among Nzinga's greatest values. She believes that people need people and it is important to be present for others and for the self. Life is a journey and Nzinga believes we must wake up each day with a renewed commitment to be and do better for ourselves and the world.

Among her accomplishments, Nzinga sites being the first person in her family to attend and graduate college among the top. She is graduate of Shaw University in Raleigh, NC the oldest Historically Black College or University in the south. Nzinga is a proud member of Delta Sigma Theta Sorority, Incorporated.

Nzinga enjoys spending time with family and friends appreciating life's journey.

When she is not writing, you can find Nzinga working in the community creating positive personal and professional experiences.

www.ingramcontent.com/pod-product-compliance
Lightning Source LLC
Chambersburg PA
CBHW021111080526
44587CB00010B/481